Choosing Binoculars for Bird Watching and Wildlife

12 essential tips to help you pick the perfect wildlife and birding binocular

by Calvin Jones

First published on Kindle in 2013

Revised paperback edition published 2017

Ireland's Wildlife, West Cork, Ireland
www.irelandswildlife.com

NB. This guide is written in British English, and as such uses British spellings. -- if you're from the USA please excuse the occasional word that looks "wrong" at first glance.

Table of Contents

Binoculars: probably the most important piece of wildlife equipment you'll ever own

While the only equipment you really need for birding and wildlife watching is your eyes and ears, most enthusiasts, and even casual observers, will agree that binoculars are pretty high on the list of must have gear.

A good pair of binoculars will enhance your experience of the natural world exponentially, revealing hidden detail and allowing you to discover and appreciate so much more of its diversity, wonder and beauty.

So you know you need a good pair of binoculars… the question is which pair do you choose?

Spoilt for choice

Not so very long ago there were relatively few options on the market when it came to buying high quality binoculars. Today the market is flooded with more manufacturers that I could list, all offering a bewildering array of models and features at a variety of different price points.

Choosing the right binoculars today can be a real headache... which is where this little guide comes in.

In it I'll explain the key things you need to look for in a birding and wildlife binocular… the critical features you need to consider when making your choice, and how you can weigh up the pros and cons to select the most appropriate binocular *for you*.

That's the real key -- picking a binocular that's perfect for you.

There's no such thing as the perfect bird watching binocular

Before we go any further let's get one thing out in the open right now: there really is no such thing as the perfect binocular. Binoculars are all about compromise… or more accurately, finding the right blend of compromises to deliver the optimum balance of weight, brightness, resolution, ergonomics and portability.

Yes, the technology is there to create a very nearly perfect optical system that works in low light and delivers stunningly pristine images… but the resulting binocular would likely be too heavy to lift, let alone carry comfortably on a hike up a mountain. It would also be eye-wateringly expensive.

So we're looking for the right balance of features and performance for birding and wildlife. A binocular that's small enough to be portable, but big enough to work well in challenging light, light enough to carry comfortably all day, but heavy enough to hold steady (more about this later) and capable of delivering uncompromising views across a whole host of field conditions.

It's a tall order… and it makes choosing the perfect binocular for you a tricky proposition.

Why I wrote this guide

As managing editor of Ireland's Wildlife I get to test a wide range of binoculars from lots of different manufacturers. I also work as a wildlife guide, and use binoculars extensively every day. Our popular Discover Wildlife Experiences on Ireland's south coast involve advising people on the choice of high quality optics, and giving them some hands on experience with the different models we have available.

Ireland -- one of the most challenging environments on earth… for a binocular

You may have heard about the Irish weather. It is *extremely changeable*.

Forget four seasons in one day, here in Ireland we can (and often do) get four seasons in one hour. And it's not just the weather that fluctuates, the light too is constantly shifting and changing.

The south coast of Ireland can be a challenging place for optics -- so it's the perfect location for putting them through their paces.

Over the years I've developed a thorough understanding of what's important when it comes to buying your ideal birding and wildlife binocular, and I get asked for advice on choosing binoculars all of the time.

People are genuinely grateful for the guidance, and because they make more informed decisions about the binoculars they buy, they end up with a better pair of binoculars that will last them for longer and enhance their enjoyment of wildlife and nature.

That is a great feeling… so I decided to write this little guide to try and help more people make the right choice when it comes to buying their perfect binocular.

The 12 tips in this guide should help you whittle down the field to a manageable shortlist of suitable candidates, and ultimately choose the right binocular for you.

1. What's perfect for me may not be perfect for you

A good quality pair of binoculars will enhance wildlife viewing enjoyment for all ages… but choosing the right pair is a very personal choice (featured model Vanguard Endeavor ED 8x42).

This first point is quite an important one. When you're choosing a pair of binoculars for birding or wildlife watching advice, reviews, opinions and guidelines will all help you to narrow down the field to a shortlist of suitable makes and models. But everybody's needs and preferences will vary, and it's important to take your own personal requirements and preferences into account.

Choosing quality optics is about finding the right compromise between size, weight, optical performance, ergonomics, practicality, function and price. Your goal is to identify the combination of features that best fits your particular needs and circumstances for your selected budget.

Recommendation: as you read through the rest of this guide keep this first point in mind. These are guidelines rather than hard and fast rules. Look to strike a balance that works well for you.

2. Budget: buy the best you can afford

Swarovski Optik makes some of the best binoculars available on the market today… but they are also among the most expensive you can buy (featured model, Swarovski SLC HD 10x42).

There's no getting around it, the very best wildlife and birding binoculars are expensive instruments, often retailing well in excess of €1,000 / US$1,500. The best-of-the-best usually will outperform most of the competition, but you pay a hefty premium for what is essentially a relatively minor (but sometimes significant) increase in performance.

There aren't too many fields today where the old adage "you get what you pay for" still hold true, but for binoculars it's still relevant to a significant degree. Precision optical instruments demand exacting standards in their production if they're going to perform at the highest level… and that precision and quality still comes at a price.

Binoculars you pick up on offer at your local supermarket for €50/€50/£50 may be OK for watching the occasional ship sail by on a sunny day at the beach, but they will fall far short of ideal when trying to pick out subtle plumage detail on a small brown bird in a shady hedgerow, or spot the tell-tale signs of distant whales blowing offshore.

Excellent binoculars don't have to cost a small fortune

Having said that the gap between the leading tier of €1,000 / $1,500 / £800 plus binoculars and some of their more affordable competition is closing. Optical technologies, techniques and components pioneered by premium European manufacturers like Swarovski and Leica have become more widely available and affordable, and production standards in more economical regions like the far east have improved to the point where manufacturers can mass-produce some remarkably capable optics.

Today you can get a good pair of binoculars for a

relatively modest investment of around €150-€200 / $200-$300 / £100-£150, and you'll find some excellent instruments in the €300-€500 / $500-$700 / £250-£400 price bracket that will serve you faithfully for decades of bird watching and wildlife observation.

Focus on value rather than price

When setting your budget for buying a pair of wildlife and birding binoculars bear in mind that buying the cheapest option available rarely delivers the best value for money in the long term. Investing a bit more will often vastly enhance your enjoyment of using your binoculars, and will get you a pair that will last you for much longer.

Look at your binoculars as a long-term investment. Unlike the latest electronic gizmos your binoculars won't become obsolete in six months, and if properly cared for the view through them won't deteriorate over time. A good pair of binoculars will keep delivering value week in week out, year after year for decades. More expensive binoculars are also made with better quality materials and to tighter production tolerances, and are built to cope with the rigours of life in the field -- which means they're built to last.

Recommendation: I always advise people to get the best pair of binoculars they can realistically afford. Binoculars are probably the most important piece of equipment in the wildlife enthusiasts arsenal, and it's almost always worth pushing the budget a bit (within sensible limits) to get a better pair.

NB. I've yet to hear of anyone who regrets spending extra money on a better pair of binoculars, but I have heard of plenty of people who wish they'd spent a little bit more… draw your own conclusions.

3. Porro-prism v roof-prism binoculars

Binoculars come in two basic designs based on the type of prism used in their optical construction — the traditional porro-prism design and the more modern roof-prism design. Until relatively recently porro-prisms were by far the most common type of binocular on the market. However as the prices for high-quality roof-prism binoculars has come down, so their popularity has increased.

Most of the top quality bird watching and wildlife binoculars on the market today are roof-prism models.

Porro Prism Binocular

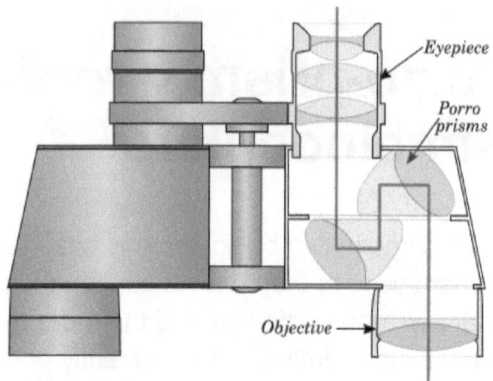

A typical Porro-prism binocular showing how the light path bends on its way through the binocular barrel (image via Wikipedia)

Porro-prism binoculars are the traditional shaped binoculars you often see featured on movies, where the smaller eyepiece lenses and the larger objective lenses are offset considerably.

Porro-prism binoculars typically share the following traits:

* Better image quality at lower price points: because of the way the optical system works porro-prism binoculars are typically cheaper to produce at any given quality point — and are therefore cheaper to buy.

* Bigger and bulkier: the porro-prism optical system tends to make binoculars much broader and bulkier than the equivalent roof-prism design — which can make them a little more unwieldy to handle in the field.

* **Less robust:** porro-prisms are typically more sensitive to damage when banged or dropped against hard objects than roof-prisms, they are also more difficult to seal, making water and dust ingress a potential problem, as well as internal fogging in extreme conditions.

Roof-prism binoculars

The more modern roof-prism design has two straight barrels with the eyepiece and objective lenses perfectly aligned — like a pair of small telescopes attached together. The result is a more compact, robust and ergonomic binocular.

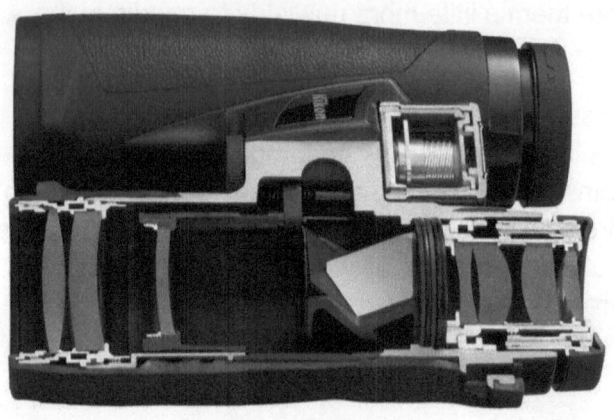

A cutaway diagram of Nikon's flagship EDG roof-prism binocular showing the straight-through barrel design and the arrangement of the different lens elements and prisms. (Image: Nikon UK)

Roof-prism binoculars typically share the following traits:

* Inferior image quality at lower price points: because roof prisms reflect light off more internal surfaces than porro-prisms, *all other things being equal* they tend to produce a darker image. They also suffer from a phenomenon known as phase-shifting which degrades the sharpness of the final image. High quality roof prism binoculars include special phase-correction, high-transmission coatings on the prism surfaces to counteract these negative effects. Roof prisms can match and surpass the quality of porro-prisms, but the performance hike comes at a price.

* More compact and ergonomic: roof prisms are typically smaller, more compact and lighter than equivalent porro-prism designs, and tend to be easier and more convenient to handle for extended periods out in the field. Don't underestimate the value of balance and handling to your overall enjoyment of using a binocular.

* More rugged and robust: roof prisms are less susceptible to mis-alignment through shock damage from impact with hard objects or surfaces. They are also easier to waterproof — and are typically nitrogen or argon purged, making them impervious to dust and water, and preventing internal fogging in extreme conditions. When the going gets tough a good pair of roof prisms will typically keep performing long after a porro-prism binocular has given up.

__Recommendation:__ if your budget is low then consider porro-prism designs to get maximum bang for your buck in terms of image quality. If you're planning to spend a little more on your binoculars then a phase-corrected roof prism design will deliver superb image quality in a more compact, ergonomic and robust package.

4. Binocular Magnification

Every pair of binoculars has two numbers printed somewhere on the instrument (usually on the face of the focus wheel, but sometimes on the body of the binocular) — for example 10×42 (pronounced ten by forty two) or 8×32. The first of these numbers is the binocular's magnification, the second is the diameter of the objective lens in millimeters (we'll get to that in a moment).

A pair of Vanguard Spirit ED roof-prism binoculars showing the magnification (8x) and objective lens diameter (42mm) clearly stamped on the face of the focusing wheel

Why more magnification isn't always better

The magnification rating tells you how much bigger the binocular will make things appear — or from a birder or wildlife enthusiasts perspective, how much closer the binocular will get you to your subject. People often jump to the immediate conclusion that higher magnification is better.

Lets quash that myth right now: it simply is not true!

While higher magnification will indeed bring things closer, and in theory will increase the amount of detail you see, it comes with a number of trade-offs that make high-power binoculars less than ideal for birding and wildlife observation.

Higher magnification tends to:

* reduce brightness, all other things being equal

* decrease depth of field (the amount of the image, from near to far, that's in sharp focus at any given point), which means you'll find yourself fiddling with the focus dial more often to keep your subject sharp

* reduce your field of view, making it more difficult to find and follow your subject effectively

* accentuate hand-shake, making high magnification binoculars more difficult to hold steady. For many this hand-shake effect will negate any increase in detail delivered by the higher magnification, and without a

support they experience a sharper image through lower power binoculars.

While the actual magnification you choose depends very much on your personal preference, the balance and handling of the binoculars you're looking at and what activity you primarily plan to use them for, the following guidelines are useful for general birding and wildlife observation:

* **12x and higher:** large magnification and lower depth of field mean binoculars of 12x and higher are typically suited to specialist long-distance viewing of subjects at a fixed distance, often from a tripod or other support to overcome the increased chance of image shake.

* **8x-10x:** considered by many to be the ideal range for general purpose birding and wildlife use, 8x-10x binoculars offer the most versatile balance of "reach", stability and image brightness for general purpose hand-held applications.

* **7.5x and lower:** can offer benefits for people who find it difficult to hold higher magnification binoculars steady, or for people who want a very wide field of view to observe fast moving wildlife (like dragonflies for example) at relatively short distances.

* **Zoom binoculars:** as a general rule *avoid zoom binoculars like the plague* — they tend to deliver inferior image quality, be less robust and generally less satisfying to use than fixed focal length optics.

Recommendation: unless you're looking to use your

binoculars for a particular specialist task choose something in the 8x to 10x range for general bird watching and wildlife observation. Try out different magnifications to see which suits you better. Generally if you're doing a lot of long distance observation (like scanning wading birds on estuaries or lagoons, for example) you may appreciate the higher magnification of a 10x. If you do a lot of wildlife watching at close quarters, or in enclosed places like woodlands trying to track small, fast-moving subjects, then the wider field of view of an 8x may suit you better.

5. Brightness

The brightness of a pair of binoculars is principally governed by their magnification (as mentioned above), the diameter of the objective lens (which dictates how much light can enter the "business end" of the binocular), and the quality of the lenses, prisms and coatings that make up the optical system.

Generally speaking the larger the objective lens, the brighter the resulting image will be, but the heavier and more cumbersome the resulting binocular will be to carry and handle in the field. As with all things when it comes to optics, choosing the right sized objective lens is about trade-offs and compromise.

* **50mm+:** larger binoculars particularly suited to low light conditions or for viewing over long distances at high magnification, often from a support.

* **40mm-50mm:** full-size binoculars considered by many to offer the optimum balance of low-light performance and portability.

* **30-40mm:** mid-sized binoculars offering reasonable brightness in a smaller, more compact frame.

* **20-30mm:** compact binoculars giving poorer low-light performance, but in an extremely portable "take anywhere" design.

What is "Exit Pupil", and how does it affect image brightness?

I've purposely stayed away from optical jargon in this guide, but "Exit Pupil" is perhaps a term that deserves a quick explanation, for the sake of clarity.

The exit pupil is the small bright disc you see if you look at a binocular eyepiece from a distance. It is the diameter of the exit pupil that essentially dictates the amount of light that can *exit* the optical system and reach the observer's eye. So a larger exit pupil means more light and a potentially brighter image.

Exit Pupil = Diameter of Objective Lens ÷ Magnification

So a 10x42 binocular has an exit pupil of 42÷10 = 4.2, while an 8x42 binocular has an exit pupil of 42÷8 = 5.25, and an 8x32 binocular has an exit pupil of 32÷8 = 4. So the 8x42 is the brighter binocular on paper, followed by the 10x42, which should be marginally brighter than the 8x32.

But the brightness of the image you see also depends on other factors, like the conditions you're viewing in.

The human pupil changes diameter from around 2-3mm in very bright conditions to around 7mm when fully dilated. If your pupil diameter is less than or equal to the exit pupil of a binocular at the time you look through it, then in theory at least the image you see should be the same brightness as seen with the naked eye.

That means that in very bright conditions you'll see little difference in brightness between different binoculars, because it's the diameter of your own pupils, not the exit pupil of the binoculars, that's dictating image brightness. Exit pupil only comes into play as conditions deteriorate and light becomes scarce.

Which to choose?

For most people a 42mm full-size binocular or 32mm mid-size binocular offers the best balance of brightness and portability in an all-round instrument suitable for extended periods of hand-held use in the field. Generally a full-size binocular will outperform a comparable mid-sized binocular in low light (early in the morning or late in the evening)… but better coatings and optical components can offset the difference and mean that high-end mid-size binoculars can and do outperform mid-price full-size binoculars, at a price.

Recommendation: choose a 42mm full-size or 32mm mid-size binocular (or similar… there are various non-standard sizes available) as your primary wildlife and birding binocular for maximum quality, versatility, convenience and comfort.

6. Optical quality

Binoculars that share the same magnification and objective lens diameter can deliver vastly different levels of optical performance. The quality of the optical components, the design of the optical system and the care and attention to detail during construction all play a role in a binocular's overall optical quality, as do the quality and application of special coatings to the lenses and prisms (see below).

The Viper HD — an outstanding high-quality binocular from US manufacturer Vortex.

Here are a few optical features it's worth looking out for when researching your new binoculars.

* ED or HD lenses: Extra-low Dispersion (ED) or High Density (HD) lenses are used in the objective lens elements of premium binoculars and spotting scopes. Their principal purpose is to correct for a phenomenon called "chromatic aberration"… or colour fringing. Colour fringing can be an issue with standard binoculars, particularly when viewing high contrast subjects (light subjects against a dark background and vice versa). ED or HD glass reduces or eliminates colour fringing, improving the perceived sharpness, contrast and colour fidelity of the resulting image.

* Edge Sharpness: all binoculars have a "sweet spot" in the centre of the field of view where the image is in sharpest focus before some loss of sharpness as you move out towards the image edge (a phenomenon known as field curvature). The wider this central sweet spot, the more enjoyable the binoculars will be to use. The better the binoculars, the larger the sweet spot, and the less softening you get as you approach the image periphery. Some premium binoculars (like Swarovski's flagship EL Swarovision range and Nikon's EDG range), incorporate special "field flattener" lenses in the eyepieces to deliver a clear view right out to the edge of the field.

* Colour fidelity: it's important that wildlife and birding binoculars reproduce colours and tones accurately. For birding in particular correct identification can depend on differentiating between subtle variations in hue. Many binoculars have a subtle colour cast. The view through them is either slightly cool (bluish) or slightly warm (yellowish or reddish) compared to the view through the naked eye. This isn't necessarily a problem as long as it's not pronounced — but look for a binocular that's as close to neutral colour reproduction as you can get.

* **Resolution:** resolution is a measure of your binocular's ability to reveal the fine detail in the subject you're viewing (individual feathers in a bird, for example), and of course a higher resolution image with more detail is *always* better (until you reach the point beyond which the human eye can't detect the difference… when it becomes purely academic). The main factors that affect the resolution of a binocular are the size of the objective lens, the magnification, the quality of the optical components and the lens and prism coatings.

* **Contrast:** the higher the contrast in the image you see through your binoculars, the better. A high contrast image will have more "snap", and makes it much easier to pick out fainter objects at distance. It also helps you to differentiate between subtle variations in tone and hue, particularly at lower light levels. Contrast is largely impacted by the quality of the lenses and prisms in the optical design, their accurate alignment to reduce or eliminate internal reflection, and of course the quality of the lens and prism coatings (again). Outstanding contrast is one of the hallmarks that gives premium binoculars that elusive "Wow!" factor.

* **Depth of field:** the depth of field is a term that

describes the amount of a scene, from near to far, that appears sharp at any given point of focus. This factor is often overlooked, but a better depth of field means less "fiddling" with the focus wheel in use, and can make a huge difference to your experience when using binoculars in the field for extended periods.

* **Close focus:** a short close-focus distance lets you view subjects that are very close to you. Most quality binoculars focus within about 3-4 metres… which is plenty close enough for most birding and wildlife. If you're interested in insects like dragonflies and butterflies, however, then you ideally want a pair that can focus to within 2 metres.

Recommendation: always strive for the best optical quality your budget will stretch to, and look for binoculars that deliver sharp, high-contrast images, with lots of detail, a large focal "sweet-spot" and good depth of field. If you're interested in watching insects pay particular attention to the close focus distance. Look out for HD or ED glass in the objective lens — but bear in mind that non-ED binoculars from premium manufacturers can, and often do, outperform ED optics from some other brands.

7. Lens and prism coatings

We've already mentioned coatings several times, and they really do transform the performance levels of any binocular. Almost all binoculars on the market today will have some kind of anti-reflective coating applied to at least some of the air-to-glass surfaces to improve light transmission, compensate for the aberrations inherent in any optical design and enhance image resolution, colour fidelity and contrast.

The quality (and expense) of these coatings varies enormously, but broadly speaking binoculars are classified according to the quality of their coatings as follows:

* **Coated:** some, but not all air-to-glass surfaces in the optical system have a special coating applied to them

* **Fully-coated:** all air-to-glass surfaces in the binocular have a special coating applied to them

* **Multi-coated:** some air-to-glass surfaces in the binocular have multiple layers of coating applied to them

* **Fully-multi-coated:** all air-to-glass surfaces in the binocular have multiple layers of coating applied to them

These days for serious birding and wildlife observation you should never consider any binocular that is not fully-multi-coated.

Anti-reflective coatings

Anti reflective coatings on the lenses and prism surfaces reduce the amount of light lost as the image passes through each surface in the optical system, improving light transmission to your eye and reducing the amount of stray light reflected around inside the binocular — thus improving image brightness and contrast.

Generally the better the anti-reflective coatings, the better the resulting image and the better the binoculars will perform across a wide range of lighting conditions. The best performing coatings are expensive to produce and difficult to apply, and typically add considerably to the cost of the finished binocular. These coatings are perhaps the main differentiating factor between premium or "alpha" class binoculars and other models.

Phase corrected prism coatings

Phase corrected prism coatings help to combat the "phase-shift" inherent in the roof prism design. They are not necessary in porro-prism binoculars.

In roof prisms the light path is split in two as it passes through the prism and then recombined, but because of the way roof prisms work the two light paths are slightly out of "phase". This reduces contrast and resolution in the the resulting image, so the best roof prism binoculars have a special coating applied to the prism surface to counteract this "phase shift" and prevent degradation of the image.

Mirror coatings

Again, these are only necessary in roof prism designs and are applied to improve the transmission of light through the prisms. In order of increasing brightness (and cost) they are:

* **Aluminium mirror coating:** typically result in light transmission of 87-93% through the prism.

* **Silver mirror coating:** result in light transmission of 95-98% through the prism.

* **Dielectric mirror coating:** a special coating technique used in very high specification binoculars to achieve >99% light transmission through the

prism.

Protective / water repellent lens coatings

These are special coatings added to the outer lens surfaces, typically of high-end premium binocular models, designed to protect the more delicate anti-reflective coatings from abrasion and damage during use and cleaning. They also usually repel water, dirt and grease, making the binoculars easier to use in the rain, and much easier to clean than binoculars without such coatings.

Recommendation: Always choose fully-multi-coated optics for wildlife observation and birding. If you're buying roof prisms look for phase corrected prism coatings and silver mirror coatings if your budget will stretch to them. Dielectric prism coatings are better, and will deliver a brighter image, but tend to cost significantly more. If you're shopping in the "premium" segment of the market, look for additional protective lens coatings that shield the external lens surfaces.

8. Field of view

Field of view is the term used to describe the extent of the scene before you that is visible when you look through your binoculars. It is usually expressed as a measurement of feet/1000 yards, metres / 1,000 metres, or as an angle of view (e.g . 110m/1000m or 6.3°).

A wide field of view is desirable for wildlife watching and birding, as it allows you to scan large areas quickly, and makes finding and following fast moving subjects (like birds) much easier.

As we've already mentioned, higher magnification tends to reduce the field of view, while larger objective lenses typically increase field of view, but also increase the bulk and weight of the binocular. Some binoculars have special wide-angle eyepieces that offer a particularly wide field of view for their configuration.

While a wide field of view is a good thing, again it often involves trade offs elsewhere in the optical design — so you're looking for a balance. The widest available field of view may not necessarily be the right choice for you.

A word about eye relief

Another term you might come across when you're

researching binoculars is "eye relief". Again, we won't delve too deeply into the technical jargon, but eye relief is basically the distance (usually specified in millimetres) between the eyepiece lens and your eye when you can see the full field of view through an optical instrument. It can be particularly important if you wear eyeglasses when using your binoculars.

If binoculars don't have enough eye relief your glasses could mean your eye is positioned too far away from the eyepiece to allow you to see the full field of view. If you want to experience the optimum view while wearing glasses choose binoculars with long eye relief (typically 16mm or longer).

Recommendation: an adequate field of view is important, but a super-wide field of view isn't really necessary, and often comes at the expense of other elements of the image that are more critical. Look for a relatively wide field of view that still delivers in terms of overall image quality. If you want to use your binoculars while wearing glasses pay attention to eye relief.

9. Balance and handling

A pair of binoculars may deliver the best image in the world, but if they're uncomfortable and inconvenient to carry and use in the field they're useless as a wildlife and birding binocular. The feel of a binocular, its weight and, more importantly, it's balance, is crucial to the overall enjoyment of owning and using it.

Binocular styles

There are three main styles of full and mid-size roof-prism binocular on the market today (porro-prism binoculars largely stick to the traditional porro-prism design, with slight tweaks — the body design is limited by constraints imposed by the porro-prism optical system):

* **Traditional single hinge:** the two barrels of the binocular are connected with a large single hinge. This is the "standard" binocular design and is the most familiar for many people.

* **Double open-hinge (also called open-bridge):** the two barrels are connected by a pair of hinges with a gap in the middle offering a "wrap-around" grip many people find more comfortable.

* **"Modern" single hinge:** offers the benefits of the open-hinge's wrap around grip, but with a single,

smaller hinge placed high on the binocular body.

Different binocular styles: "modern" single hinge (Swarovski SLC HD — left), traditional single hinge (Vanguard Spirit ED — centre) and the popular open-hinge design (Hawke Frontier ED — right).

Different styles suit different people. My personal preference is for the modern single-hinge design, followed by the traditional single hinge and finally the double open-hinge design that has become so popular today (a trend pioneered by the popular Swarovski EL series, and since adopted by several other manufacturers).

Weight

Lightweight is good, particularly if you're going to be carrying your binoculars for long periods of time, but it's important to remember that lighter isn't always better.

High quality optical components are generally far weightier than low-quality equivalents. Quality lends high-end binoculars a solid feel and "heft" when compared to their cheaper counterparts. That weight is reassuring, and with a well balanced design it can make the binocular easier to carry and hold steady for longer periods.

Be wary of binoculars that feel almost too light for their size — the weight savings often come at the expense of quality.

Feel and balance

A well balanced binocular should feel natural in your hands, and should almost become an extension of your body once you get used to it. Your binocular should become a seamless interface between you and the scene you're viewing — so natural you almost forget it's there.

> **Bottom line:** if you have to think to use your binoculars then you have the wrong pair of binoculars.

> **Recommendation:** balance and handling is a very personal thing, but you should be able to get some idea of what the binoculars on your shortlist are like by reading reviews online from people who've spent time with the binoculars you're considering. Try searching birding and wildlife forums (like Bird Forum) for recommendations by owners — and try

and get to use as many different types of binocular as you can to see how different models and different styles feel to you (see point 12 Try Before you Buy).

10. Build quality and durability

Build quality is another one of those crucial areas when it comes to a precision optical system. High performance optics require painstaking manufacture within extremely tight tolerance limits to deliver consistent levels of quality in the finished product. The slightest misalignment of any component in the construction can seriously affect the performance of the binocular.

Again, you tend to get what you pay for here to some degree, and optics from established top-flight brands are usually incredibly well made (my Swarovski binoculars are still the best made piece of equipment I have ever owned). That said there are plenty of very well made binoculars in the low-to-mid range from manufacturers who take quality every bit as seriously as the premium brands.

Binocular housing / body and rubber armour

Durability is critical when you're making a significant financial investment in a product. Most wildlife and birding binoculars employ a high-strength housing that holds and protects the internal optical system and gives the binocular it's shape, heft and balance.

These housings typically consist of the following materials:

* **Polycarbonate:** light, strong and relatively low cost, high strength polycarbonate bodies are typically used in many budget- to mid-range binoculars

* **Aluminium alloy:** light and strong, many manufacturers employ aluminium alloys in the construction of their mid- to high-range binoculars

* **Magnesium alloy:** the strongest and lightest weight material currently used for binocular housings, typically used on premium models from high end optics manufacturers, although there are exceptions.

In addition to the main metal or polycarbonate housing, most modern binoculars will have a protective rubber armour applied to both protect the binocular from minor impacts and to improve grip and handling in the field. Some housings and armour feature sculpted or textured surfaces to help with grip and balance.

Waterproofing and sealing

For wildlife watching and birding you really want a binocular that is completely waterproof to give you piece of mind when using your optics across a wide range of conditions. Most roof prism binoculars on the market today that are suitable for birding and wildlife are waterproof, and are purged with an inert gas (either nitrogen, or less often argon) to drive out water vapour and eliminate the potential for internal fogging when moving between extreme temperature gradients (from a warm car onto a wintery moorland, for example).

Waterproof binoculars don't just guard against rain and wet — they also ensure that dust, sand and other dry particles can't find their way into the binocular — which can be just as important.

Recommendation: make sure the binoculars you buy are robust enough to stand up to the rigours of extended field use. Choose a lightweight but sturdy pair, with good balance and grip and always make sure they are fully waterproof and nitrogen or argon purged.

11. Warranty

The Vortex Optics Unlimited Lifetime No-Fault VIP Warranty is about as good as binocular warranties get.

Your binoculars represent a significant investment — and you want a pair that is going to serve you well for many years. One useful guide to the longevity of a pair of binoculars is the type of warranty offered by the manufacturer. While not infallible, this at least gives you a steer on the manufacturer's confidence in the quality of their product.

Typical warranties for high quality binoculars last from 10 years to 30 years depending on the manufacturer and cover any faults in materials and workmanship for the duration of the warranty.

A few manufacturers offer lifetime warranties with

their products, and some even go as far as offering an unlimited lifetime warranty with a "no-fault" clause, which means the manufacturer will repair or replace the binoculars completely free of charge for any defect or damage, however caused, for the lifetime of the product.

The Vortex Optics VIP Warranty is an example of this — and is one of the most comprehensive binocular warranties I've ever seen.

Recommendation: *while few people will buy binoculars solely on the strength of a warranty, and hopefully you won't need to avail of it, a manufacturer's willingness to stand over their product is obviously a major plus. Focus on features and the overall quality of the binocular first — but do consider the warranty in the "mix" before making your final selection.*

12. Try before you buy

It's not always possible to try all of the binoculars on your short-list before you make a decision. In many places high quality optics retailers are thin on the ground, so finding somewhere that stocks the models you're interested in can be a challenge. That said there really is no substitute for experiencing the different views, handling and features of a range of different binoculars to give you a "feel" for which options suit you best.

Here are some suggestions on ways you can get to try different optics out before you buy them:

* **Optics retailers:** if you're lucky enough to live near a major optics retailer head to the store and try out a range of different binoculars. If possible try to use the binoculars outdoors, rather than under the artificial lights of the store.

* **Shows and events:** events like the UK Bird Fair (or something similar near you) have stands from most leading optics manufacturers keen to demonstrate their latest models. They are the perfect place to use a wide range of different optics outdoors in field conditions.

* **Trips and outings:** attend outings, trips and guided walks organised by your local bird club or wildlife group, and ask other people if you can try out their binoculars. Most people are more than happy to oblige, and you can get a good idea of how different

models at different price-points perform in the field.

* **No-quibble returns:** given how difficult it can be to get "hands on" time with high-quality optics in some places, some mail order companies (particularly in the US — but increasingly in Europe) offer a no-quibble return policy, allowing you to order with confidence, try the binoculars for a short period, and then return them for a full refund if you're not happy with your purchase, no questions asked.

Recommendation: try to get your hands on as many different binoculars as you can before deciding on which pair to buy. The perfect binocular can be a very personal thing, and there really is no substitute for actually trying a variety of models to see what works for you.

Conclusion

There's a lot to consider when choosing a new pair of birding and wildlife binoculars. I hope this guide helps you to weigh the various pros and cons and pick out the perfect option for you. Above all I hope your new binoculars help you to have many more spectacular and memorable wildlife encounters over the coming years.

Please take a moment to leave a review

If you've found this little book useful please do consider heading back over to Amazon and leaving a review to let other people (and me) know what you think.

About Calvin Jones

Calvin Jones is a lifelong wildlife lover, founder and managing editor of Ireland's Wildlife (www.irelandswildlife.com), and wildlife guide on Discover Wildlife Experiences on the stunning West Cork stretch of Ireland's Wild Atlantic Way.

He started Ireland's Wildlife to share his passion, and encourage more people to engage with the natural world around them. It has the added bonus of allowing him to head outside with a pair of binoculars and legitimately claim he is working.

Originally from the North Wales coast, Calvin now lives in an old schoolhouse in rural West Cork, Ireland with his wife, three daughters and 8 chickens. Living in the country was supposed to be peaceful, but so far it's not working out that way....

You may also like

Bridwatching for Beginners
A short, simple guide to help you take your first steps in a hobby that can last a lifetime

Empire: Book One of the Bantara Chronicles
Empire is a tale of heroes and tyrants, assassins and spies that unfolds against a backdrop of civil unrest and political intrigue. It follows one woman's quest to unearth her true heritage, unlikely alliances and a chain of events that change the fate of the mighty

Empire of Bantara forever.

Visit www.irelandswildlife.com